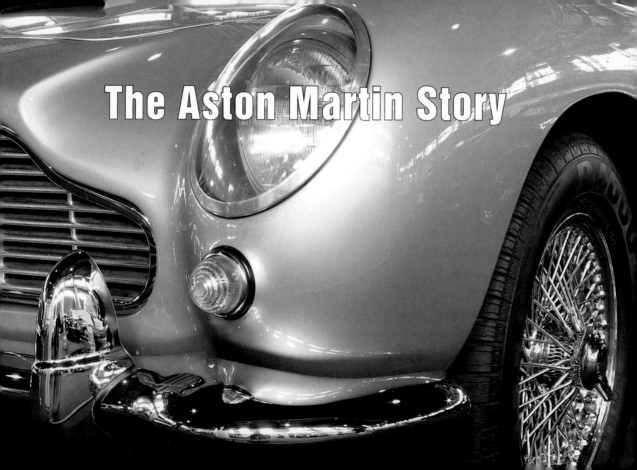

The Aston Martin Story

The Aston Martin Story

John Christopher

The History Press

Published in the United Kingdom in 2012 by
The History Press
The Mill · Brimscombe Port · Stroud · Gloucestershire · GL5 2QG

British Library Cataloguing in Publication Data
A catalogue record for this book is available from the British
Library.

Hardback ISBN 978-0-7524-7133-4

Typesetting and origination by The History Press
Printed in India

Half title page: Up close and personal with
the iconic DB5. (Shutterstock)

Half title verso: Rear-end evolution – DB2,
DB4 and DBS GT. (JC)

Title page: Side vent and slash
detail. (JC)

CONTENTS

I am grateful to the dedicated and talented photographers whose images are included in this book, including: Shutterstock, Alexandre Prévot, Garrymichaelsmith Dreamstime.com, DavidF, Brian Snelson, Les Chatfield, David Merrett, Louis Rix, epfennig, Brian Snelson, Ed Callow, Arend Vermazeren, daveoflogic, Autoviva.com, Rundvald, Jagvar, Jayt1980, Simplexvir, Razbox, SoulRider.222, Jay Christopher, Ellesmere FNC, Nicolas Garcie, Marcin Okupniak Dreamstime.com, Ballo84, El monty and Hatsukari715. Photographs by the author are credited as JC.

In addition I must thank Amy Rigg of The History Press for letting me write about my dream cars, and my wife Ute for her support and proof reading.

John Christopher, 2012

Aston Martins are truly special – they always have been and always will be.

Dr Ulrich Bez, CEO Aston Martin Lagonda

Guaranteed head-turners, instantly recognisable in a sea of automotive blandness, the great Aston Martins are the sexiest things on four wheels – and if you think I am only talking about the classic models of the 1950s and 1960s then just take a look at the more recent offerings such as the stunning One-77. Not that this was of any interest to me and my fellow generation of schoolboys, of a certain age, who delighted at the flicking of a tiny plastic villain out of the roof of Corgi's golden-coloured diecast. Why Aston Martin never offered an ejector seat as an optional extra on the real DB5 is beyond me to this day. Nonetheless the James Bond connection has been priceless, both

◀ The famous Aston Martin wings on a DB2. (JC)

for Aston Martin and countless enthusiasts, and for many of the latter it was more than enough to cement a life-long love affair with the marque.

Above all else the Aston Martin story is one of survival against the odds. While other top-end independent British car companies such as Jensen and Bristol have gone the way of the dinosaurs – marques of extinction – other smaller manufacturers such as Morgan have carved their own niche in the market. Yet Aston Martin, or strictly speaking Aston Martin Lagonda Ltd as it is nowadays, weathered the storm to be reborn time and time again. It has

◀ The great escape of 2011 – William and Katherine depart from Buckingham Palace in the DB6 Volante owned by Prince Charles. (Garrymichaelsmith Dreamstime.com)

▶ Wire-wheel detail, DB6. (JC)

done so under a succession of different owners from the original founders Robert Bamford and Lionel Martin – there never was a Mr Aston – to the post-war era under David Brown's leadership and the later, often turbulent years of consortium and corporate ownership.

The key to this longevity is to be found in the cars themselves. Yes they are expensive, but they are beautifully expensive. Aston Martin has produced a long line of models, sports cars or at least sports-car inspired, that can only be described as 'drophead gorgeous' while performing like racing thoroughbreds. As we approach the marque's centenary in 2013, the Aston Martin brand is stronger than ever and the latest catalogue offers the largest and most diverse range of models ever seen. Sometimes described as Britain's Ferrari, the Aston Martin marque is more than a world leader, it is a legend.

> Bond had been offered the Aston Martin or a Jaguar 3.4. He had taken the DB III. Either of the cars would have suited his cover – a well-to-do, rather adventurous young man with a taste for the good, the fast things of life.
>
> Ian Fleming, *Goldfinger*, 1959

The first car to bear the Aston Martin name was the 1915 'Coal Scuttle' produced by two friends, the engineer Robert Bamford and sporting motorist Lionel Martin. The duo had come together to compete in hill climbs using a modified Singer and they decided to launch their own business, Bamford & Martin, in 1912, initially to sell Singer cars, as well as servicing GWK and Calthorpe vehicles, but with the intention of building their own cars. There never was a Mr Aston, that part of the name coming from the famous hill climb at Aston Hill near Aston Clinton in Buckinghamshire. At their premises in Kensington, Bamford and Martin created the first car by fitting a four-cylinder Coventry-Simplex engine on to the chassis of a 1908 Isotta-Freschini. But the outbreak of the First World War interrupted their plans to start production and the company folded.

After the war Bamford & Martin was revived and a second prototype was finally completed in 1920, by which time Robert Bamford had moved on. A funding injection came from the flamboyant American Count Louis Zborowski, who is still remembered for his legendary Chitty-Bang-Bang special, a pre-war Mercedes chassis powered by a massive 23-litre Maybach aero-engine.

Zborowski's backing enabled the production of a series of light cars with 1.5-litre, four-cylinder side valve engines, on short and long chassis in a variety of body styles, ranging from two-seater race and sports cars to four-seater tourers or saloons. Unfortunately Count Zborowski was killed in the 1924 Italian Grand Prix and although car production for Bamford & Martin had been steady, with around sixty sold, it was not enough to prevent the factory closing and with it the departure of Lionel Martin in 1925.

In 1926 Aston Martin Motors Ltd was formed with backing from the Charnwood family. At the helm were Bill Renwick and Augustus Bertelli, who had worked in partnership to develop an overhead cam 1.5-litre four-cylinder engine which they had planned to sell to an existing car company, but sought instead to build on the Aston Martin brand name by creating

a car for their engine. With Augustus Bertelli as technical director, and his brother Enrico's coach-building shop situated right next door, a series of models emerged from the new works at Feltham from 1926 until 1937 and these have become known as the 'Bertelli cars'.

THE BERTELLI CARS

Three new Aston Martin models were launched at the 1927 Motor Show at Olympia, London; the four-door T-type saloon and tourer, both on a 9ft 6in (2.9m) wheelbase chassis, plus the shorter S-type sports car. A keen racer himself, Bertelli was

committed to 'improving the breed' through participation in national and international motor racing. Accordingly the company had its own series of team cars starting with the 1928 Le Mans 1 and 2, or LM1 and LM2. Neither finished the race but they did provide the basis for Aston Martin's next production model, the International, introduced in 1929. Its sporting credentials were evident in the under-slung chassis, overall low profile, and the motorcycle-style mudguards which hugged the front wheels and turned with the steering. A variety of bodyworks were available including two, three and two/four-seater saloons and tourers. And, in 1931, near replicas of the team cars were produced as the International Le Mans (not to be confused with the later Le Mans model).

Priced at £598 for the four-seater saloon version, the International was not a cheap motorcar for its class or its time, and even though the range was well received Aston Martin continued to struggle financially. The 1929 Wall Street Crash further undermined the high-end car market and by 1932 the company needed bailing out once again. This time backing came from L. Prideaux Brune and shortly afterwards ownership passed on to Sir Arthur Sunderland.

The next series of 1.5-litre cars, produced between 1932 and 1933, included the New International. This was built on a new chassis and, in order to keep the price down, it also incorporated a number of components from other manufacturers. The New International was the first model to wear the iconic Aston Martin wings badge, and the radiator had changed from a previous flattened front to a slight V. Only twelve examples of this stop-gap model were sold as it was quickly superseded by the Le Mans in October 1932. As the name suggests, the Le Mans was a sporty thoroughbred

◀ First Series, produced between 1927 and 1932. (DavidF)

Did you know?
There never was a Mr Aston in Aston Martin. The name came from the Aston hill climb in the Chilterns and was selected because it put the company near the front of alphabetical listings.

inspired by the successes in the classic Le Mans 24 Hour race. It had a more powerful 70bhp engine and a lower business-like appearance created by a low-set radiator and bonnet line. A four-seat sports version was added to the range in 1933. The Le Mans was extremely successful, with more than 100 built. Running concurrently with the Le Mans, a 'standard' car was offered on a longer 10ft (3m) chassis. It was known as the Standard 12/50 and was available in tourer or saloon body work, but only around twenty examples were produced.

The Mark II unveiled at the 1934 Motor Show was basically an improved version of the Le Mans. The engine was a little more powerful, producing 73bhp, and once again it was available in two chassis lengths – for either two- or four-seaters – in saloon, tourer, drophead coupé or sporting saloon versions. Stylistically the Le Mans retained the motorcycle style mudguards, and beneath the winged badge the radiator shutter was thermostatically controlled. The two-seater had a top speed reported as 85mph (137km/h) with the windscreen folded down.

For the 1934 racing season Aston Martin had three team cars, LM11, LM12 and LM14, but no LM13 for superstitious reasons, all based on the Mark II. These were two-seaters with a sloped tail space accommodating the spare wheel stowed on its side. None completed the Le Mans, although LM11 and LM12 were rebuilt and entered into the RAC Tourist Race in Ulster. Resplendent in a new coat of red paint to replace the British Racing Green which Bertelli considered to be unlucky, they came first, second and third in their class and Aston Martin won the team prize. Accordingly the Ulster name stuck and in 1934 a 'replica' version was packaged for the public as an amateur racer's car

with a not unreasonable £750 price tag. Twin carburettors boosted its horsepower to 85bhp with a top speed around the 100mph (160km/h) mark.

THE 2-LITRE RANGE

Building on the success of the 1.5-litre models, 1937 saw the launch of Aston Martin's new 2-litre range, and also the departure of Bertelli following a fall-out with the new owners. Aston Martin's road cars were still on the expensive side and by introducing the more powerful engine while keeping the cost at about the same level it was hoped to make them more competitive. The 1.5-litre engine was modified and enlarged to 1949cc and first used in the team cars entered in the 1936 Le Mans, although in the event the race was aborted because of industrial action. However, despite this setback, twenty-three production versions were marketed as the 2-litre Speed Model between 1926 and 1938.

These appeared with a wide variety of body styling from different coach-builders, as was customary at that time. The last of these, the C Speed or Type C model, was produced in 1938 to use up the remaining unsold chassis. The eight Type C cars featured accentuated streamlining and an extenuated pointed rear end.

➤ Only one pre-war Atom was made, but this bulbous car was to play an important role in shaping the future of the marque. (Louis Rix)

The main application for the 2-litre engine was the 15/98 range which was shown at Olympia in 1936 and made available as either the two- or four-door 15/98 Tourer or the Saloon. The 15/98 number refers to the RAC rating combined with the 98bhp output. An advertisement published in *Country Life* in 1936 sang its virtues:

Amazing performance equal to most 4-litre cars – at the running cost of a 2-litre! Experienced motorists who try these cars invariably say, 'I never knew a 2-litre could accelerate like this.' Remember also Aston Martin reliability – three times winners of Rudge Cup, Le Mans 24 Hour race, and many other successes.

The Short Chassis Coupé was offered at £525, the Long Chassis Saloon at £495 and the Tourer at £495. A short chassis 15/98 drophead coupé was launched in 1937. This had a 'dicky seat' at the rear for an extra passenger, but the model was not especially popular and only twenty-five were built.

With the coming of the Second World War, car production ceased as the company concentrated on war work, mostly producing parts for Vickers. However, this was not before the prototype of the Atom had made its appearance in 1939. This curvaceous car, intended as a new model to replace the 15/98, was revolutionary in its use of lightweight square-section tubing for the frame, plus its independent front suspension and aluminium aerodynamic body. Initially it was fitted with the 15/98's trusty 2-litre engine, but this was later replaced by a new four-cylinder 2-litre engine designed by Claude Hill. The war came too soon for the Atom to enter production, but the car was to play an important part in shaping generations of Astons to come.

This car has a nature like an angel. So responsive you can accelerate from zero to 100 mph and back in under twenty-five seconds. So docile and forgiving, your control and mastery of every situation is supreme.

Aston Martin advertisement for DB4 Vantage, 1963

In 1946 the Sutherland family decided to put the Aston Martin company up for sale. Their advertisement in *The Times* caught the eye of David Brown, whose engineering company, founded by an earlier David Brown, produced gears and farm tractors. Brown went to Feltham to see what was on offer, borrowed the Atom and in February of 1947 he personally bought the company for £20,500. By coincidence the luxury car maker Lagonda was about to be wound up and, interested in their W.O. Bentley-designed 2.6-litre engine, Brown acquired Lagonda for £52,500. The two concerns were brought together and Brown skilfully combined the best elements from each to create a new series of superb cars numbered and immortalised by the use of his own initials, 'DB'.

2-LITRE DB1

The first car to emerge from the Feltham works after the war and under the ownership of David Brown was the Aston Martin 2-litre Sports, otherwise referred to, but only in retrospect, as the DB1. Its chassis was a stretched version of the Atom's – with a longer wheelbase of 9ft (2.7m) – and had rear coils instead of leaf springs. In July 1948 the prototype won the Spa 24 Hour Race and this 'Spa Special' was displayed at the London Motor Show alongside the standard model. In production only briefly, from 1948 to 1950, it was a stylish drophead with a provocatively long bonnet and luxuriously sweeping wings. It had the feel of a Lagonda, not surprisingly as this car was the progeny of Lagonda's designer Frank Feeley, albeit laced with the genes of the pre-war Atom. And while the slippery bodywork was clearly all post-war, the stiff upright radiator grille harked back to earlier more formal times. In the innocuous small horizontal grilles to either side – a not uncommon feature for this period – the seeds were sown for the shape that would evolve into Aston Martin's signature nose piece. Behind the grille lurked Claude Hill's 2-litre four-cylinder engine, putting out an acceptable 90bhp and up to 93mph (150km/h). However, only fourteen examples were produced before it was time to hand over to its successor.

DB2 AND DB2/4

The DB2 looks like an Aston Martin should. It combines that essence of good looks, a muscular bodywork and the promise of power beneath an elongated bonnet. More than any other car the DB2 set in

▼ DB2 grille and badge. (JC)

motion the evolutionary process that has resulted in its modern counterpart. The DB2 was derived from one of the three cars entered in the 1949 Le Mans 24 Hour race. Designed around the tube-frame chassis created by Claude Hill for the 2-litre Sports DB1, and finished with a closed coupé body by Frank Feeley.

Technically the DB2 was a massive advance on the 2-litre car. It had the 2.6-litre Lagonda engine, a straight-six with overhead cam designed by W.O. Bentley and William Watson. Top speed was around 116mph (187km/h) and acceleration from 0–60mph (97km/h) was in 11.2 seconds. The DB2 was first seen at the New York Auto Show in April 1950 and 411 of the cars had been produced by the time of its retirement in 1953. After the first forty-nine cars the triple front grille was morphed into a one-piece with horizontal slats. A drophead coupé version of the

▲ DB2 Coupé at the Haynes Motor Museum, although unusually for them not in red. (JC)

an optional engine with larger carbs and higher compression ratio pistons was made available as Aston's first Vantage upgrade. And some cars returned to the factory to have later 3-litre engines fitted.

If the DB2 had been good, then Aston Martin made sure that the DB2/4 was even better. Closely based on its predecessor, the DB2/4 had had a number of cosmetic enhancements including wrap-around windscreen, bigger bumpers and less drooped front wings with repositioned headlights. At first it had the same Lagonda engine, and for later versions of the drophead and saloon a 2.9-litre version was introduced, upping the power to 140bhp and the top speed to 120mph (193km/h). This made the car an ideal candidate for the competition scene and in 1955 three works cars were entered in the 1955 Monte Carlo Rally, and two for the Mille Miglia. The DB2/4 also launched Aston Martin's screen

DB2, introduced in the latter part of 1950, proved very popular with over 100 built and accounting for around one quarter of all DB2 sales.

The DB2 was extremely successful in racing and lent itself to several variants including the first Vantage, built for racing driver Briggs Cunningham. From 1951

Did you know?
In 1961 David Brown attempted to revive the Lagonda brand with the four-door Lagonda Rapide based on the DB4. The Rapide name was later revived, in 2010, for the latest four-door Aston.

career when a drophead coupé appeared in Alfred Hitchcock's 1963 classic *The Birds*.

A Mark II introduced in 1955 accommodated an optional large-valve high compression engine churning out 165bhp. Visually there were a few tweaks including small tail fins – a hint of things to come – new tail lights and more shiny chrome.

The Mark II also saw a transfer of the coach-building from Feltham to Newport Pagnell and the Tickford Coachbuilding Works which David Brown had purchased in 1954. The DB2/4 proved to be the most successful Aston Martin so far with 764 built by the time the model was phased out in 1957.

DB MARK III

Not the DB3 (see 1950s Racers opposite), the DB Mark III is more usually referred to just as the Mark III. To me it was the best-looking Aston of the 1950s. It was produced for a relatively short period from 1957 until 1959, but in that time 551 were built. It was very much an evolution of the DB2/4 but with the wider open-mouthed grille and the Lagonda 2.9-litre engine's output raised to 178bhp with an optional dual-exhaust system. This reduced the 0-60 acceleration time to just 9.3 seconds. The

mid-level DBD engine could conjure up 180bhp, while a handful of high-spec cars fitted with the optional high-output DBB engine possessing three twin-choke Weber carburettors, long-duration camshafts and high-compressions pistons, took the power output to a hefty 195bhp. Coupé variants of the Mark III were also produced, including drophead and fixed-head coupés.

THE 1950S RACERS

As an offshoot of the company's production models and works racing cars, a clutch of sleek purpose-built racing cars emerged from the Feltham stable during the 1950s. The first of these, the Aston Martin DB3, was introduced in 1951 and although it sported the Lagonda 2.6-litre straight-six used in the DB2 Vantage its performance failed to impress and the engine was replaced by a larger 2.9-litre engine the following year. On the track it produced mixed results, coming first, second and fourth behind a Jaguar C-Type at Silverwood, all three cars retiring from the 1952 Le Mans,

before romping home to an overall win at Goodwood's nine-hour race. Between 1951 and 1953 ten DB3s were built, with five used as works cars and the others sold to individuals who wanted to go racing.

▼ Ready to race, 1952 DB2, PUM 6, photographed at Silverstone Classic 2011. (David Merrett)

It was succeeded by the DB3S, basically a lighter version of the DB3, which was in production for three years from 1953 until 1956. Watson squeezed more power out of the 2.9-litre engine and eventually raised the output to 240bhp. The car also had fabulous curvy bodywork designed by Feeley, notable for its gaping 'egg crate' grille. Thirty-one were built, out of which eleven were works cars and these enjoyed considerable success with a string of victories, including wins at Silverstone in 1953, 1954 and 1955, plus Goodwood in 1953, 1955 and 1956. Only Le Mans eluded the Aston Martin team and this situation was put right by the DBR1 which came on the scene in 1956.

Changes to the rules to sports car racing meant that they no longer had to be road-legal and the DBR1 was the first pure

➤ The ultra-sleek DBR1 which brought Aston Martin's greatest victory at the 1959 Le Mans. Photographed at Goodwood Festival of Speed in 2009. (Brian Snelson)

first time there were triangular vents on either side – a design feature handed down to successive generations of Astons. Its first powerplant was a 2.5-litre racing version of the Lagonda straight-six, but this was replaced by the more powerful 2.9-litre engines. The DBR1 amassed an impressive collection of race trophies, including Goodwood in 1957, 1958 and 1959 and at the Nürburgring in 1959. But the icing on the cake was 1st and 2nd place at Le Mans in 1959 and, later that same year, winning the World Sportscar Championship. The DBR2s of 1957 were similar to the DBR1 in appearance, but were made using two chassis built for the short-lived Lagonda project known as the DP166.

Aston Martin ended the decade at an all-time high and victory on the race track was matched by a new series of modern sports cars heralding the golden years of the 1960s.

◀ Double triumph in 1955 at Silverstone and Spa.

racer. Chief designer Ted Cutting honed the DB3S's bodywork down to an even lower profile. It had an oval mouth and for the

A car for connoisseurs – the Aston has many virtues and few faults.

Road & Track magazine, Mark III review, 1959

The DB4 was a ground-breaking model for Aston Martin. First unveiled at the Paris Motor Show in 1958, followed by a British début in London, this was a completely new design and the first of the Astons to be built at the company's Newport Pagnell works in Buckinghamshire. Its continental flavour was courtesy of the sizzling bodywork by Carrozzeria of Milan wrapped around a 'superleggera' – Italian for 'super light' – framework, or cage, of small diameter tubing. While it captured an element of the former models it had an unashamedly modern shape that established the flavour of the 1960s Aston Martins. This included the full range of signature motifs with a slightly flattened grille having indented top corners, the bonnet scoop and the side vents with their chromium-plated go-faster slashes.

The DB4's chassis was brand new and its 3.7-litre engine had been designed by Aston's Tadek Marek as a dual overhead cam straight-six with cylinder head and block of cast aluminium alloy. Admittedly there were some issues with overheating in the early examples, but even so according to Aston Martin the twin-SU carburettor version produced 240bhp, acceleration from 0–60mph in 9 seconds and a maximum speed of 140mph (225km/h).

During its production between 1958 until 1963 the DB4 was available as a coupé or drophead and underwent several changes

◄ A stunning example of the DB4. (Ed Callow)

➤ Before Bond burst on to the scene, Corgi Toys offered the no-gadget DB4, beautiful in red.

CORGI TOYS

TRADE MARK REGISTERED

OPENING BONNET
ENGINE · SEATS
SPRING SUSPENSION

2 1 8

ASTON MARTIN D.B.4

through its five Series models. For example, the Series 1 cars had a rear hinged, front opening bonnet and plain bumpers without vertical over-riders. On the first fifty cars the side windows were frameless, resulting in unwanted wind noise at speed and so window frames were added. The Series 2, introduced in 1960, had uprated brakes, the bonnet was hinged at the front and the rear quarter lights, those small triangular side windows, were made to open. In the engine compartment the cooling sump was enlarged and the oil pump uprated, while an oil cooler with scoop under the bumper was an optional extra.

The Series 3 cars had few external differences apart from a change to the rear light clusters which came from the Humber Hawk and had been inherited from the old Mark III. In contrast the changes on

the Series 4 were mostly cosmetic with the introduction of the grid-like barred grille and a flattened bonnet scoop. The final Series 5 was lengthened by 3.5in (9cm), the roof was raised to provide extra passenger space and to compensate for this the diameter of the wheels was reduced by 1in (2.5cm). Other minor changes were made

to the rear and front indicators, the boot handle grew bigger and attached itself to the top of the rear number plate.

The DB4 Vantage was launched in 1961 and even though the first ones were based on the Series 4, most Series 5s were built

to Vantage specs with an additional third carburettor, plus larger cylinder valves and raised compression ratio. To thoroughly confuse the Aston Martin spotter the Series 4 Vantage and Series 5 models are virtually identical to the casual observer. Furthermore the faired-in headlights on the Series 4 Vantage and later Series 5 vehicles are commonly mistaken for the DB5 or DB6.

DB4 GT AND ZAGATO

The GT was a lightweight high-performance version of the DB4 with a thinner aluminium body, reduced wheelbase and specially modified 3.7- or 3.8-litre engines to raise the output to 302bhp and the max speed to 151mph (246km/h). Seventy-five DB4 GTs were restyled by Ercole Spada of Zagato and these have been rightly described by Tim Cottingham of astonmartins.com as being 'probably the most beautiful cars

of all time and certainly the greatest road going Aston Martin'. Lighter and with an upgraded engine the Zagato offered up 314bhp and a top speed of 153mph (246km/h). Twenty cars were produced, but the phenomenon of Zagato-envy has seen a handful of sanctioned replicas and a number of unofficial Zagato make-overs. If the DB4 GT Zagato looks incredibly modern from an early twenty-first-century

◀ The later three-light rear cluster on a DB4 photographed in London. (Ed Callow)

▼ The DB4 GT Zagato is arguably the most beautiful car ever. Only nineteen were built and this 1962 example in Caribbean Pearl was shown at the Geneva Motor Show in 2011. (Autoviva.com)

perspective it is because it continues to inspire so many of today's automotive designers.

DB5

Perhaps the greatest legacy of the DB4 is that it gave the world the DB5. In many ways this model can be viewed as an ersatz Series 6 DB4, but in a masterful stroke of good luck and clever marketing Sean Connery's James Bond made this the most instantly recognisable car in the world. So what makes the DB5 different to its predecessor? The engine was enlarged from 3.7 to 4.0 litres fitted with three SU carburettors to produce 282 bhp and 145mph (233km/h), plus a new ZF five-speed transmission. Intended as a luxury grand tourer, the DB5 was offered as a coupé, convertible and, in limited numbers, a shooting brake or estate car, each with two doors and four seats. The interior

For you, a possession that reflects immaculate taste and rare discrimination. Of nearly two million British cars produced annually, Aston Martin account for just three a day. Each painstakingly hand-built by master-craftsmen . . . true devotees of the marque. The DB5 is the fastest regular 4-seater G.T. car in the world. Top speed exceeds 150 m.p.h. Stops from 100 m.p.h. in 6 seconds. Murmurs through traffic and arouses interest everywhere. Experience the ultimate in high-performance motoring — DB5 ASTON MARTIN.

Aston Martin built 4 litre light alloy engine, 282 b.h.p.; twin overhead camshafts; 3 carburettors; micronic air-filter; oil cooler; 5 speed all synchromesh gearbox, top overdrive; power assisted discs; alloy body shell mounted on light tubular structure and carried on steel platform safety chassis; luxuriously appointed; air conditioning optional. Also available with the Vantage engine as an alternative; 3 Weber Carburettors developing 325 b.h.p.

Aston Martin Lagonda Ltd., Newport Pagnell, Bucks. Tel: Newport Pagnell 720. London Showrooms: 96/97 Piccadilly, W.1. Tel: GRO 7747

featured reclining seats, carpets, electric windows and full leather trim. The exterior look was finished off with chrome wire

▲ Descended from the DB5, the DB6 presents a familiar countenance, but details such as the split bumper aid identification. (Brian Snelson)

wheels, although little refinements such as extending tyre slashers, machine guns and an ejector seat were only optional extras for one particular customer.

The DB5 Vantage appeared in 1964 with a number of engine mods to produce 315bhp, but only sixty-five were built. The DB5 convertible – the Volante name had yet to be coined – were made available from 1963 through to 1965, and a handful of these had the DB6 Vantage spec engine. Thirty-seven convertibles based on the DB5, but referred to as short chassis Volantes in comparison with the longer DB6, were made in 1965 and 1966.

In total just over 1,000 DB5s were built, but perhaps the most surprising thing about it is that this iconic vehicle was only in production from 1963 until 1965.

DB6

▼ The DB6 six-cylinder in-line engine with three SU carbs. It looks like a piece of sculpture or jewellery. (JC)

The DB6 tends to be overshadowed by its more showy predecessor. Produced from 1965 until 1971, it actually had the longest run of any Astons to date and in that time almost twice the number of DB6s were produced than had been the case with the DB5. The DB6 was a new model even though it does bear a close resemblance to the DB5. The main visual differences were a 3.75in (9.5cm) increase in wheelbase, revised profile including a raised roof-line, steeper windscreen and the flattened rear end with lip-spoiler to reduce aerodynamic lift for increased stability at speed, plus split corner bumpers. Power steering and air conditioning were optional. The DB6 was powered by Tadek Marek's 4.0-litre twin-overhead camshaft in-line six-cylinder engine, and the Vantage option raised the standard from 314bhp to 325bhp. Top speed was 150mph (241km/h). The DB6 Volante was introduced at the London Motor Show in 1966 to replace the existing short chassis Volantes based on the last DB5s. A total of 140 were built including twenty-nine Vantage versions.

A Mark II, launched in 1969, had fashionable flares on the wheel arches, wider wheels and, as an optional extra, AE Brico electronic fuel-injection. Probably the most famous DB6, a Volante Mark II in dark blue, was the car given by the Queen to Prince Charles as a twenty-first birthday present. He has since had it converted to run on bioethanol fuel and recently it was driven by his son, Prince William, as the Royal Wedding going-away car in 2011.

By the end of its run in 1971 the DB6 was like the party guest who has outstayed their welcome. The 1950s-inspired styling was a

little long in the tooth, the 1960s had come to a close and the popular taste for classic retro was still a couple of decades away in the future. For the 1970s it was a case of out with subtlety and in with big, brash power machines.

> Having the front nearside wheel blasted off the Aston Martin Volante by the police does not hinder Bond and Kara's escape plans. With the aid of a rocket motor, ski outriggers and a 45° incline the Aston Martin becomes airborne, astonishing the Czech border patrol guards.
>
> 'The Living Daylights', *The Official James Bond Movie Book*, 1987

In many ways the 1970s and 1980s can be viewed as the middle period for Aston Martin – a bridge between the heights of the 1960s sports cars and the more recent return to stylish curves. That's not to say that these were fallow years, although the company did go through many changes and difficulties, but the emphasis in terms of design was placed on the need to modernise. The result was a period epitomised by big squared-off bodywork leading, at its extremes, to the low-profile wedges which represent on the outer edge of the Aston Martin spectrum.

➤ The next generation of Aston Martins was characterised by wider and squarer bodies. This is the 1969 DBS. (Rundvald)

DBS, V8, VANTAGE AND V8 VANTAGE

The foundations of the next generation were laid in the latter part of the 1960s, in particular with the launch of the DBS in 1967. This was the successor to the DB6, although the two models ran concurrently for three years. The DBS saw the DB6 chassis widened by 4.5in (11.5cm) and the wheelbase lengthened by an inch (2.5cm). However, the overall length of the body designed by William Towns was actually slightly shorter than its predecessor. Even so, there was ample room inside this two-door coupé for four comfortable seats. At the front, the bonnet had lost its trademark

aston martin V8

Aston Martin curved corners in favour of a more modern squared-up grille, although the bonnet scoop and the side gill vents were still present. As the new V8 engine was not ready in time the DBS was fitted with the same 4.0-litre engine as the DB6, and at no extra cost the customer could opt for Vantage tuning with Italian-made Weber carburettors to up the output to 325bhp. Top speed of this heavy car was respectable enough, in the region of 140mph (225km/h).

In 1969 the DBS was the chosen car of the latest 007, George Lazenby, in *On Her Majesty's Secret Service*. Unlike Connery's DB5s this vehicle displayed only the barest minimum of gadgets – see *Now Pay Attention, 007…* – however, the combination of a fresh actor and car marked a new era for both Bond and Aston Martin. A 'Bahama Yellow' DBS was also driven by a future Bond, Roger Moore, as Lord Brett

V8 brochure cover.

Rear view of the DBS.
(Rundvald)

Sinclair in the 1971–1972 television series
The Persuaders.

Production of the DBS ceased in 1972
with a total output of 787 cars. That same
year David Brown sold the firm to Company
Developments Ltd. The replacement for
the DBS, the DBS V8, had already been
available for three years by this time. Its

5.3-litre V8 engine upped the bhp to around the 315 mark, and it could accelerate to 60mph (97km/h) in 5.9 seconds, reaching a top speed of almost 160mph (257km/h). The newly engined car was described as 'staggeringly powerful'. By April 1972, when the six-cylinder DBS was dropped, the DBS V8 became known simply as the Aston Martin V8. It was available as a hard-top or Volante model and there were several 'Series' with variations in engine and transmission.

In 1977 the Vantage name was revived. Usually this was used as a suffix to imply an improved version of a particular model, but between 1972 and 1973 it was a distinct model in itself. Visually the Aston Martin Vantage resembled the standard model apart from wire wheels and single headlights, but the old straight-six engine was seen as a retrograde step and this so-called 'entry-level' Aston failed to attract customers with only seventy-one produced. Thankfully the V8 Vantage went some way to restore the balance. It looked like the old DBS or V8 apart from some minor differences – the bonnet scoop was closed off and an integral spoiler was added at the rear with another under the nose to handle the extra speed. There had been some tinkering with the engine – revised camshafts, larger inlet valves and crabs – and Aston claimed that performance had been improved with a top speed of 170mph. The V8 Vantage was a popular model and continued in production until 1989. Sales reached 534, no doubt helped by an appearance as the latest gadget-laden Bond car in *The Living Daylights*, starring Timothy Dalton as 007's fourth incarnation. Would that make him version 007.4 nowadays?

◀ 1976 V8 Vantage in Royal Cherry. (Jagvar)

V8 ZAGATO

Once again Zagato applied its styling to an Aston Martin, this time the V8

with a coupé, and later a convertible, but unfortunately their magic dust had lost some of its lustre and the result is a somewhat pedestrian-looking vehicle with uninspiring angular bodywork. Even so the name was enough of a draw and eighty-nine were sold between 1986 and 1990. The Zagato was powered by a 430hp V8 engine with twin-choke Weber carbs and a top speed of 186mph (300km/h). The

British comedian and petrol-head Rowan Atkinson bought the first right-hand drive version and had it modified for racing.

VIRAGE 1989–2000

Despite the fact that the Virage continued in one form or another until 2000, and for much of that time was produced concurrently with the DB7, visually it looks like an evolutionary throwback. This is hardly surprising as the Virage had been conceived in 1986 as the successor to the V8 range which, like an ageing film star, was beyond the reasonable stage for further facelifts. Presented at the Birmingham Motor Show in 1988, the two-door four-seat Virage had a hand-built body of aluminium alloy mounted on a modified version of the Lagonda chassis. A big car, its revamped 32-valve 5.3-litre V8 engine ensured it had the performance of a sports car with a top speed of 155mph (249km/h). Stylistically some commentators have described the Virage as elegant, with many references to the curves and proportions of the DB4, but for many Aston Martin aficionados the end result is just that bit too bland. And in a cost-cutting exercise many components, including the headlights and tail lights, steering column, dash switches and so on, had come from other car companies. A Volante model was made available from 1992 onwards, and this was followed by the first shooting brake to be produced in-house, along with only four examples of an extended wheelbase four-door Virage known as a Lagonda Saloon.

The restyled and more rounded Virage Vantage was produced between 1993 and 2000, and the later models were known just as V8s. With twin superchargers the 5.3-litre engine had a staggering power output of 550bhp and a top speed of 200mph

◄◄ 1986 V8 Vantage Volante, on display at a USA Concours show with non-standard wheels. (Jagver)

◄ The 1998 Vantage coupé in black. All very elegant, but perhaps not Aston's finest hour. (Jayt1980)

THE LAGONDA CONNECTION

Between 1961 and 1964 David Brown had attempted to revive the Lagonda marque with the Lagonda Rapide, a four-door GT largely based on the DB4. The Rapide had a 4.0-litre straight-six engine, later used in the DB5, but its styling looked heavy-handed in comparison with the lither Astons and only fifty-five of the expensive made-to-order vehicles were produced.

▲ Virage Vantage, skirted and spoilered. (daveoflogic)

➤ The long-nosed Aston Martin Lagonda sold well, but is it aristocratic or just plain ugly? (JC)

(320km/h). One limited edition of forty V8 Vantage Le Mans came out in 1999, and the final Virage derivative was a limited-edition nine-vehicle run of V8 Vantage Volantes in 2000 to mark the end of car production at the company's Newport Pagnell works.

Did you know?

Bond's V8 Volante, seen in the early scenes of *The Living Daylights*, was actually owned by Aston Martin Lagonda chairman, Victor Gauntlett. Later scenes in the film feature a pair of V8 saloons.

In 1974 another Lagonda briefly appeared on the scene, a four-door saloon based on the existing V8 design, although 1ft (30.5cm) longer to provide greater passenger space for the luxury car market. The Series 1, as it became known, was an expensive car and only seven were built. It was succeeded by a radical new Lagonda design, the Series 2, which was unveiled at the 1976 London Motor Show. Its unconventional ultra-modern appearance was in stark contrast to the other cars. Described as 'stunning' by some critics, you either love its wedge-shape styling or you hate it. Either way, you can't ignore it. The Series 2 Lagonda was based on the Aston Martin V8 chassis, and beneath that plain bonnet was a lively 5.3-litre V8. Early models featured a flat digital instrument panel and touch-pad controls, plus a steering wheel that would not have looked out of place in a Gerry Anderson creation. Otherwise the interior styling was decidedly old-school traditional with brown leather and lots of wood trim. For the Series 3, of 1986, fuel injection was introduced together with cathode ray instruments, and later on a fluorescent display system, to replace the digital instrument panel. The 1987 Series 4 saw the corners rounded off and the pop-up headlights gave way to conventional lights on either side of the tiny grille.

A number of non-standard variants of the Lagonda appeared including extended Tickford-bodied long-wheelbase limousines, a two-door shortened version known confusingly as the Rapide, and a single shooting-brake or estate car. Production of the Aston Martin Lagonda ceased in 1989 after 645 had been built.

THE BULLDOG

Following the favourable reception of the Lagonda, Aston Martin's most extreme foray

◄ Rare Aston Martin Lagonda shooting brake. (Simplexvir)

into the wedge profile came with the Bulldog, a concept vehicle with styling attributed to William Towns, and development work by Mike Loasby who went on to work for DeLorean. The Bulldog was produced as a one-off in 1979, although the original intention had been to build a limited run of twenty-five. Its design features included many that are common to the wedge-shapers; low-profile – only 43in (1.1m) high, concealed headlamps, a large sloping windscreen, gull-wing doors and a rear-mounted engine. This was a 5.3-litre twin-turbo delivering up to 700bhp and it was anticipated that the Bulldog would achieve a sizzling 200mph (322km/h), although in tests it managed only a verified 191mph (307km/h). Inside, the dash had the fibre-optic liquid-crystal type instrumentation developed for the Lagonda.

The aluminium bonnet runs all the way to the leading edge of the car, accentuating the apparent power of the car. We wanted the DB9 to look like it was milled from a single, solid piece of aluminium.

Henrik Fisker, Aston Martin Designer

The DB7 is held in very high esteem by Aston Martin enthusiasts for several reasons. Firstly, it saw a return to the David Brown DB numbering system. Secondly, it was the so-called 'entry-level' model that saved the ailing Aston Martin marque and carried it into the twenty-first century. And thirdly, it was a damn fine car. Even *Top Gear*'s Jeremy Clarkson pronounced that the DB7 was No.1 on his list of the most beautiful things built by man, ever. So it must be true.

It had been Aston Martin's former chairman, Victor Gauntlett, who had first recognised a need for an Aston that would be smaller and cheaper than the big hand-built V8s. Something that would sell in volume. The opportunity to make this move into the wider market came about following the Ford Motor Company's purchase of Aston Martin in 1988. Ford also owned Jaguar and resources for the NPX project, as it was known, began to take shape with the DB7's platform derived from the Jaguar XJS and adapted from the cancelled Jaguar F-type – the XJ41 coupé and XJ42 convertible – designed by Keith Helfet. Ford recognised that if they had pushed ahead with the F-type it might have taken away the lion's share of Aston Martin's market.

Acclaimed as the saviour of the marque, the Aston Martin DB7 arrived in 1993. (Alexandre Prévot)

Instead the F-type design was applied to the XJS platform with Aston Martin design refinements added by Ian Callum – according to some the modern equivalent of Michelangelo. Seen from the perspective of the later, more muscular, steroid-enhanced models, the DB7 looks understated, almost too polite. But placed in the context of the chunky slab-bonneted DBS and V8 Virage era, then the DB7 can be appreciated for what it is. With sensuous, sculpted curves Callum's design was a breath of fresh air with more than a passing nod to Aston Martin's glory days. It was nothing less than a work of art on four wheels. And if it bears a family resemblance to the Jaguar XK-8 it is hardly surprising as that car also uses an evolution of the XJS/DB7 platform.

The prototype DB7 was completed by November 1992 and its unveiling at the Geneva Motor Show in March 1993 was greeted with universal acclaim. The DB7 went into production in 1994 at a new factory acquired at Bloxham, near Banbury in Oxfordshire, which had previously been used to make the big but short-lived Jaguar XJ220 supercar. DB7 production was unique for Aston Martin

as it was the only model built with steel unit construction inherited from Jaguar, instead of the aluminium used for the chassis and most body parts of the other later models. A Volante version followed

▼ Externally the DB7 Vantage looks like the standard DB7 apart from the revised side lights. (JC)

▲ DB7 Vantage in profile – a close relation of the Jaguar. (JC)

in 1996. Both models had a 24-valve twin-cam straight-six 3.3-litre engine with water-cooled Eaton supercharger, developing a respectable 335bhp and 361lb ft (489 N m) of torque, and a top speed of 155mph (250km/h). For owners who craved a little more oomph, a Driving Dynamics package of enhancements was provided.

DB7 V12 VANTAGE AND GT

The DB7 really came into its own with the unveiling of the first ever twelve-cylinder Aston Martin, the V12 Vantage, at the London Motor Show in 1999. This sported a 6.0-litre 48-valve V12 engineered by Ford Research and Vehicle Technology Group together with Cosford Technology. It was first seen in a Ford concept car and the Lagonda Vignale before it found a place in the DB7 Vantage. The DB7 V12 had a hefty 420bhp at its disposal, was available with either six-speed manual or five-speed automatic gearboxes, and the manual version had a top speed of 186mph (299km/h). Sales were strong and consequently by mid-1999 the original straight-six model ceased production.

An improved variant of the DB7 Vantage, known as the GT, or GTA if equipped with automatic transmission, appeared in 2002, promising even greater performance with the bhp raised to 435, increased driver involvement and enhanced road handling. Minor changes to the bodywork included a wire mesh front grille, two bonnet vents and a spoiler on the boot, plus new rear vented disc brakes by Brembo. This was the

▼ DB7 Vantage.
(daveoflogic)

▲ The Zagato-styled
DB7. (Brian Snelson)

car that really got Clarkson's juices flowing. After demonstrating its ability to pull away and attain 135mph (217km/h) in fourth gear he gleefully concluded that the DB7 might be 'cramped, old and expensive, but it is epic fun!'

◄ A rare pair – the Zagato DB7 together with the DB AR1 roadster. (Jagvar)

Did you know?
Despite its quirky looks with a long, flattened bonnet, the Aston Martin Lagonda was popular with many customers and a total of 645 were produced between 1976 and 1990.

He wasn't alone in liking the car. Just over 7,000 were manufactured at the Bloxham plant by the time it was superseded by the DB9 in 2004, far in excess of all other models up to then, equalling the combined number of Aston Martins ever produced.

It has been universally acclaimed as one of the most beautiful cars ever built and is justifiably epitomised as the favourite first model for many Aston owners.

SPECIAL EDITIONS AND VARIANTS

In addition to the standard models a number of special editions and variants of the DB7 were also produced.

The 1998 Alfred Dunhill Edition consisted of 150 platinum metallic DB7 i6 models, and later that same year ten special black cars were made for the Neiman-Marcus Christmas catalogue. Also in 1998 six midnight blue cars, two coupés and four Volantes, were produced as the Beverly Hills edition. The following year the Stratstone Edition featured nineteen special black cars; nine coupés and ten Volantes. The DB7 V12 Vantage appeared in 2002 in the Keswick Limited Edition 'Nero Daytona black'. The 2003 Jubilee Limited Edition saw sixty 'Jubilee blue' cars made for Europe and the USA to mark the Queen's Golden Jubilee, although I can't help thinking that they should have been in gold and not blue. Also in 2003 a special Anniversary Edition of 'slate blue' cars was announced to mark the end of DB7 Vantage production.

There were two variant models produced towards the latter stages of the DB7s production. The DB7 Vantage Zagato saw a return to the type of styling panache not seen since the DB4 GT Zagato of the early 1960s. Appearing for the first time at the Paris Motor Show in October 2002 it had the more rounded nose with bigger curved grille and signature double-bubble roof, plus a re-styled rear end. The DB7 Vantage Zagato was offered as a limited production of only ninety-nine cars which sold out immediately, with one additional example produced especially for Aston Martin's own collection. Built on a wheelbase 2in (5cm)

◀ Styled by Zagato the DB AR1, standing for American Roadster 1, was produced without a roof for the American market. (JC)

shorter than the standard DB7 and a body length a full 6in (15.25cm) shorter, this two-seater grand tourer was available as either a coupé or convertible. Power was supplied by a 6.0-litre V12 engine with manual transmission, producing 0–60mph acceleration in 4.9 seconds and a top speed of 186mph (299km/h). The modified DB7 chassis was built in the UK and shipped to Zagato in Milan for the hand-fitting of the aluminium body panels.

The direct successor to the DB7 Vantage Zagato was the DB AR1, produced by Aston Martin and Zagato specifically for the USA market – in particular for customers in Florida and California – the AR1 name standing for American Roadster 1. Introduced at the Los Angeles Auto Show in January 2003 only ninety-nine were produced, all of which were open topped without a roof of any sort. In the event all but eight went to American customers, the others remaining in Europe. (Only two were produced to a right-hand-drive layout.) The DB7 Vantage Zagato was not available in the USA because of strict safety rules requiring re-testing of the model as a new car. Instead the DB AR1 was based on a standard DB7 Vantage Volante chassis, and accordingly it should not be regarded merely as an open-top version of the DB7 Vantage Zagato. Stylistically there is a close family resemblance, especially at the front, but for obvious reasons the double-bubble motif has migrated from the non-existent roof to the rear to serve as roll protection. Both cars had the 6.0-litre V12 from the Vanquish, and on the DB AR1 the manual version had a slight advantage over the automatic in terms of speed and acceleration.

◀ The rear humps of the distinctive DB AR1. This right-hand drive version is on display at the Motoring Heritage Centre which is next door to Aston Martin's Gaydon facility. (JC)

> With its taut dimensions, flared arches and ground hugging stance, the handsome design has an aggressive, sporty look unspoiled by gimmicky decoration.
>
> Julian Rendell, V8 Vantage report, *Autocar* magazine, January 2003

Having re-established the reputation of the Aston Martin marque, and after almost ten years in production, it was time for the DB7 to hand over to a new generation of models. And it just so happened that they were even better.

V12 VANQUISH

Designed by Ian Callum, the V12 Vanquish is said to resemble his previous car, the DB7 in its Vantage manifestation. The V12 Vantage began life as Project Vantage, a concept car powered by a 450bhp 6-litre V12 which had been intended for the abandoned Lagonda Vignale and, in theory at least, was capable of more than 200mph (322km/h). Reaction to the concept car was favourable enough for Aston Martin to develop a production version and as the Vanquish this was unveiled at the Geneva Motor Show in 2001.

Beneath the aluminium skin panels there was a framework consisting of a strong aluminium and carbon composite bonded monocoque. Power was supplied by a 48-valve 6.0-litre V12 producing 460bhp and a max speed of 190mph (306km/h). Gear change was via an F1-style paddle. The Vanquish was available as a two-door, in either two- or four-seater, but an open-top or Volante version never made it into production. To maintain model differentiation, once the DB9 had been launched in 2004 the Vanquish was uprated with new suspension and an improved engine output of 514bhp.

In 2002 James Bond returned to the Aston Martin fold with the appearance, and disappearance, of the Q-pimped Vanquish in Pierce Brosnan's last outing as 007, *Die Another Day* (see *Now Pay Attention, 007*...). The Vanquish S was launched in 2004, increasing power for a top speed of 204mph (328km/h) and incorporating sportier suspension and handling, plus some styling revisions including new wheels, altered nose, raised boot and a larger spoiler with integral brake light.

To commemorate the end of the Vanquish, and of car production at Newport Pagnell, the Vanquish S Ultimate Edition consisted of forty 'Ultimate Black' cars, but with manual gearbox and transmission in place of the much criticised paddle.

THE ULTRA-COOL DB9

The Aston Martin DB9 marks the start of the Gaydon era with car production based at the new purpose-built Warwickshire plant beside the former V-bomber airfield. The DB9 sports car was the natural successor to the DB7 and Ian Cullum's input is evident although its design was completed by his successor, Henrik Fisker. In interviews Fisker stated that the DB9 should look as if it had been milled from a single piece of aluminium. With no sills, drain channels or visible bumpers, it has an altogether smoother and less aggressive appearance than the Vantage. Launched in 2004 the DB9 was the central model in Aston's three-tiered range, positioned between the entry-level V8 and the top-end Vanquish. The DB9 range included coupé or Volante variants. *Top Gear* decided the DB9 was actually 'too cool' for its famous cool wall and placed it in its own mini-fridge.

In engineering terms it is the first in Aston Martin's VH – Vertical/Horizontal – platform which utilises a commonality of components and still allows for different length chassis. This explains why the current models all look similar to each other. The incredibly strong body structure is composed of lightweight aluminium and composites melded together by self-piercing rivets and robotic-assisted adhesive bonding. The

Ultra smoothie, the DB9 Volante photographed in the USA. (SoulRider.222)

Aston Martin DB9. (Alexandre Prévot)

engine is the same as in the V12 Vanquish, the 6.0-litre V12. Some changes were made in 2008 including an even more powerful engine, modified gearbox, redesigned interior centre console along with a minor external facelift including new front grille, mirrors and choice of wheel designs. More tweaks were planned for 2011.

V8 AND V12 VANTAGE

Launched a year after the DB9, the V8 Vantage, known simply as the V8 at first, was intended to dig into Porsche's traditional 911 market. The motoring press dubbed it the 'Baby Aston' and priced initially at under £80,000, *Autocar* magazine heralded the arrival of the V8 as 'the most affordable Aston ever'.

The two-seater coupé has a bonded aluminium structure for lightness and strength. Power came from the 4.3-litre 32-valve V8 originally, but models

produced after 2008 have the bigger 4.7-litre V8. From 2006 the car was also offered as a convertible known as the V8 Vantage Roadster. It's a little heavier than the coupé but said to deliver the same sizzling performance. Over 10,000 V8s

have been sold so far, a figure only matched by the DB9.

Then came the V12 Vantage in 2009. Based on the V8 Vantage and developed from a concept car first shown in 2007, this has the V12 engine from the DBS, achieving 510bhp and a top speed of 190mph (310km/h). There's a new rear diffuser, retractable rear wing, carbon-ceramic brakes, plus carbon-fibre boot lid and bonnet to save weight. The car can be distinguished by its extra bonnet vents and the unusual shaping of the lower nose section which spreads like a pair of splayed table legs to either corner.

In 2011 Aston Martin released the V8 Vantage S, in both coupé and roadster versions, for a more sporty driving

◀ No flashy badges on the rear view of the Vantage. Owning one is enough of a statement in itself. (daveoflogic)

◀◀ V8 Vantage Volante. (Alexandre Prévot)

◀ V12 Vantage with a cluster of bonnet grilles. (Jay Christopher)

Did you know?

The appearance of 007's Vanquish in the 2002 film *Die Another Day* earned it the number three spot in *Autotrader's* list of 'Best Film Cars Ever'. The DB5 from *Goldfinger* and *Thunderball* came first.

experience. This has been achieved by fitting Sportshift II transmission, a seven-speed gearbox, tuning the engine to deliver 430bhp, stiffened suspension and uprated brakes. Aerodynamic enhancements include a deeper front bumper with carbon fibre splitter and larger tailgate lip.

DBS V12

Reviving the DBS name, Aston launched the new DBS V12 in 2007. The engine is the same as in the DB9. Built at the Aston Martin engine plant in Cologne, Germany, it is a big 5.9-litre 48-valve V12 with six-speed manual, or optional automatic, transmission. This churns out 510bhp and achieves 0–62mph in a very fast 4.3 seconds. Max speed is 183mph (295km/h).

◄ 'Darling, shall we take your Aston or mine?' Belgravia, London, 2011 style. (Ed Callow)

Aston's Adaptive Damping System (ADS) alters the suspension to raise the control levels as set by the driver, or to deal with road or weather conditions. When ADS is selected the throttle and braking response is increased and the steering sharpened. Extensive use of carbon fibre, most notably in the bonnet, boot and doors, keeps the weight to a minimum – a saving of 66lb (30kg) compared with the DB9. Likewise

◀◀ DBS full-frontal. (JC)

◀ DBS in the showroom. (JC)

The Volante version features an electrically controlled roof which can be lowered in fourteen seconds at the press of a button. Special editions include the Carbon Black and the UB-2010, the latter named after company chief executive Dr Ulrich Bez. Inevitably Bond got his hands on the DBS in the 2006 *Casino Royale* and again in the pre-title car-smashing chase around Lake Garda for 2008's *Quantum of Solace*.

At the time of publishing, the DB9, the V8 and V12 Vantage, as well as the DBS, are all currently in production at Gaydon.

▲ DBS Volante, gloriously black. (Alexandre Prévot)

the brakes are carbon ceramic to further reduce weight. The carbon fibre content continues in the interior with the carpets specially produced from thin layers of the material. 2+2 seating is offered as an option.

A factory pumping out up to 5,000 cars a year – its best ever. And maybe a motor sports programme. Car enthusiasts everywhere ought to thank Uli Bez and Ford for giving Aston Martin its brightest future for years.

Autocar magazine, September 2003

Following the successes experienced by the works cars in the late 1950s, culminating with spectacular wins at Le Mans and the World Sportscar Championship title in 1959, Aston Martin set its sights on the Formula One World Championship. Unlike the previous progressive development of its sports cars, their first Formula One car, the DBR4 designed by Ted Cutting, looked every inch like a racing car, but beneath the surface its chassis was a conventional spaceframe structure closely related to the DB3S sports car of 1956. The suspension had double wishbones with coil springs and telescopic dampers at the front, and a torsion bar system at the back, but by the time the DB3S had made its début at the Dutch Grand Prix in 1959 most of the other manufacturers had already put their cars on all-round independent suspension. The layout of the BDR4's single-seat narrow body was typical with the driver positioned near the rear wheels and the engine shoe-horned into the slender nose. This was the familiar Tadek Marek straight-six, naturally aspirated and sleeved to reduce its capacity to 2.5 litres and an output claimed at 280bhp. However, when put to the test the car's less than ideal aerodynamics and frequent engine failures did not bring the

Did you know?
Aston Martin's greatest year on the race track was 1959 when their works cars won the Le Mans 24 Hours race and the Sports Car World Championship.

hoped-for Formula One glory. For the non-championship BRDC International Trophy race at Silverstone two cars were entered, driven by Roy Salvadori and Carroll Shelby, who finished in second and sixth place. A promising enough start but not followed in their World Championship performances with the cars taking part in only five of the 1959 series. The following year an improved DBR5 appeared on the scene, a smaller and lighter version of the DBR4 with all-independent suspension, but the results didn't come and accordingly Aston Martin withdrew from Formula One.

Returning to more familiar territory the DP212 sports car was built for the 1962 Le Mans. Based on the DB4GT chassis with modified suspension, longer bodywork and a 4.0 litre straight-six with twin overhead cam developed from Tadek Marek's 3.7 litre engine. At the 1962 Le Mans, driven by Graham Hill and Richie Ginther, it began well, taking the lead at the start but gradually falling back to ninth place before retiring after seventy-nine laps. Slightly modified, with a revised rear spoiler, it was prepared for a return to Le Mans in 1963, but in the event its place was taken by the newer DP214 and DP215.

The DP214 was also based on the DB4GT chassis, with a new body design and the smaller Tadek Marek 3.7-litre straight-six

The DAVID BROWN
ASTON MARTIN
DB3S Competition Car
Race-bred from a line of International successes

THE DAVID BROWN CORPORATION (SALES) LIMITED

ASTON MARTIN DIVISION · FELTHAM · MIDDLESEX · *London Showrooms: 103 New Bond Street W.1*

◀ The DB3S Competition Car – 'Race-bred from a line of international success.'

was forced to retire on the sixtieth lap after a piston failure, and DP215 achieved fifth place by lap 110 before suffering the same fate. After that Aston Martin dropped out of racing and the two DP214 cars were sold at the end of the 1963 season. One crashed the following year during practice at Nürburgring, killing the driver Brian Hetreed. The other was entered in the 1964 Le Mans but disqualified nearly eighteen hours into the race after a breaking of the rules determining when the oil could be replenished.

AMR1

The ensuing hiatus was only interrupted in 1989 with the arrival of the Aston Martin AMR1. This was a Group C formula car developed by Proteus Technology Ltd (Protech), a partnership between Aston Martin and the Scottish racing firm Ecurie Ecosse. The AMR1 was a state-of-the-art

this time. The lone DP215 built alongside the DP214 was lighter and had the benefit of the 4.0-litre straight-six, although it had originally been earmarked to receive the 5-litre V8. At the 1963 Le Mans the DP214

racing machine incorporating a monocoque carbon-fibre and Kevlar body designed by Max Bostrom and a mid-mounted 6-litre V8 designed by Reeves Callaway and derived from Aston's 5.3-litre units from the V8 Virage. Known as the RDP87, Callaway's

engine put out 600bhp and could achieve a top speed of 217mph (350km/h).

Five AMR1s were built but the cars' racing debut began badly when AMR1/01 was severely damaged in Japan during preparations for the first race in the World Sports Prototype Championship. Two cars were entered in the 1989 Le Mans but

◀ 1970s Aston Martin V8 with droop-snoop. (Brian Snelson)

◀ DBR9 in Gulf colours and with 007 racing number. (daveoflogic)

◀◀ Team Odena DBR9 at Gaydon. (JC)

◀ V8 Vantage N24 being race-prepped. Note the roll cage. (daveoflogic)

comparatively under-powered they ran in the mid-field and only AMR/01 completed the race in eleventh place. By the end of the season Aston Martin was sixth in the Teams Championship and development of the AMR2 for the 1990 season was already in hand when Protech became bankrupt and the company closed in February 1990.

A NEW BREED OF RACING CARS

At the start of the twenty-first century Aston Martin had reaffirmed its position in the luxury sports car market and with renewed confidence announced a return to motor racing. In 2004 they formed a partnership with the Prodrive engineering group to form Aston Martin Racing. The DBR9 was a heavily modified variant of the highly successful DB9 road car. Naturally it inherited some of the DB9's good looks, and retained the chassis, V12 engine block and cylinder heads, but otherwise

it has been re-engineered for maximum performance. All body panels, with the exception of the roof, are constructed from carbon-fibre composite to save weight. The body has enhanced aerodynamics, a flat bottom and a rear wing to optimise down-force. The result is a car that rockets from 0–60mph (100km/h) in a breathtaking 3.4 seconds. Debuting in 2005 the DBR9 won the Sebring 12 Hours in its category, and came a respectable third in the Le Mans.

Aston Martin Racing currently runs four DBR9s in the top GT1 class, and the DBRS9 has been produced in the GT3 class to provide a more affordable alternative for other motorsport teams. The Vantage N24 was introduced in 2006 as a GT4 class racing car based on the V8 Vantage. This has a front splitter, extended door sills for great aerodynamic efficiency, roll cage and a stripped-out interior to meet race specifications. A single Recaro driver's seat

and polycarbonate windows help to keep the weight to a minimum.

In 2009 Aston Martin announced a full works entry in the Le Mans Prototype category with the Lola Aston Martin B09/60. Aiming to emulate their Le Mans victory of fifty years earlier the programme got off to a bad start when one car was wrecked during pre-season testing. Two more cars were entered but one was involved in a collision with a GT1 Aston and the other was retired after 252 laps. The 2011 successor to the B09/60 is the AMR-One which features a downsized 2-litre engine to meet new regulations for endurance racing. Two cars entered in the 2011 Le Mans were dogged by bad luck, one retiring after only two laps and the other achieving just four before returning to the pits. This caused Aston Martin Racing to announce that they were 'easing' development of the AMR-One to focus on their GT racing programme.

◄ Lola Aston Martin in action. (Nicolas Garcie)

The first four-door Aston to make it into production is an instant hit. It's less aggressive than most of the company's two-seaters, but still an Aston Martin at heart.

What Car? Review of the 2011 Aston Martin Rapide

▼ At the start of the twenty-first century the marque has attained new heights. (JC)

Thanks in no small part to Aston Martin's HV – Horizontal Vertical – engineering platform the latest range of models is the largest in the company's history. The current catalogue (2012) lists fifteen: the DBS Coupé and Volante, the DB9 Coupé and Volante, the V8 Vantage Coupé and Roadster, the V8 Vantage S Coupé and Roadster, and the V12 Vantage – all mentioned in previous chapters – plus some newcomers including the One-77, the V12 Zagato which is due to hit the tarmac in 2012, the four-door Rapide, the Virage Coupé and Volante and, finally, the diminutive Cygnet.

ONE-77

This two-door coupé has been described as insane, a super-supercar with a price tag to match – a tidy £1.2 million. Planned as a limited run of just seventy-seven exclusive

The sizzling One-77. It will set you back a cool £1.2 million. (Marcin Okupniak Dreamstime.com)

cars, hence the name, its first appearance was at the 2008 Paris Motor Show. Designed by Marek Reichman, the One-77 almost defies superlatives. An Aston Martin with attitude, the full-on styling stretches the marque's usual features into a wide-mouthed grimace. It is absolutely stunning! But in this instance beauty is more than skin deep and squeezed under its slanting bonnet is the naturally aspirated 7.3-litre V12 offering 760bhp. According to Aston this is the most powerful naturally aspirated engine in the world. The One-77 uses a strengthened version of the DB9's six-speed automated manual transmission and height-adjustable suspension with dynamic stability control. Top speed is thought to be over 200mph (320km/h) with a very fast 0–60 in about 3.5 seconds. And if you want one you had better hurry as by mid-2012 they were nearly all sold.

V12 ZAGATO

If you need to tighten your purse strings a little then the new V12 Zagato is a very pretty alternative to the One-77 at about one-third of the cost. Fifty-years after the DB4 Zagato the V12 version has all the hallmark features, but beefed up with some sharp styling resulting in deep side indentations, a wide mouth and the meanest of sloping rear ends. Only 150 will be built and deliveries were scheduled to start in late 2012.

RAPIDE

Introduced in 2010, this four-door sport saloon derives its name from the Lagonda Rapide of the 1960s, despite the fact that the last four-doorer was actually the wedge-nosed Aston Martin Lagonda of the 1970s and '80s. The new Aston Martin Rapide is based on the DB9 with a lengthened wheelbase. A review in *Car* magazine said,

➤ 2011's Virage, an Aston with attitude. (JC)

Did you know?
With a price tag of a cool £1.2 million, the One-77 is the most expensive Aston Martin production car ever produced. Despite that, there has been no shortage of customers.

'This is Aston Martin being sensible. Well, relatively sensible.' The engine is the same as in the DB9, the 6.0 litre V12 for 470 bhp, and 0–60mph (100km/h) in a very respectable 5 seconds, plus a top speed of 188.5mph (303km/h). Unlike the rest of the Aston Martin cars the Rapide is built at the Magna Steyr production plant in

Graz, Austria. At first it was anticipated that 2,000 would be produced every year, but the global recession had dented the market for a luxury four-door saloon and this figure was cut to 1,250 by June 2011 and is likely to go lower still.

◄ A sheep in sheep's clothing, the Cygnet runabout is based on the Toyota iQ. (El monty)

CYGNET

Compared with its sleek stablemates the Cygnet is Aston Martin's ugly duckling. This three-door two-seater hatchback is a rebadged version of Toyota's iQ city car. The Cygnet has a restyled nose with

Virage grille detailing. (JC)

Aston Martin grille badge and vents, plus miniature side-vents and a reworked, more luxurious interior, but that's about all you get for the extra £18,000 or so above the basic iQ's on-the-road price. Even so, Aston Martin have high hopes for the Cygnet which was added to its range in 2011 in order to comply with new European Union regulations for fleet average emissions.

2012 VIRAGE

After the jaw-droppingly beautiful specials, and the city-slickers' Cygnet, it is only proper to conclude this account of Aston Martin with the very latest production car, the Virage. It's an old name but there's nothing dated about the new 6-litre V12-engined coupé introduced in 2012. It sits nicely between the DB9 and the DBS both in terms of performance, price and styling. In other words it is another highly desirable thoroughbred from the Aston Martin stable.

> For you, a possession that reflects immaculate taste and rare discrimination. Of nearly two million British cars produced annually, Aston Martin account for just three a day. Each painstakingly hand-built by master craftsmen...
>
> Aston Martin advertisement for the DB

James Bond and Aston Martin – a marriage made in heaven. The suave and sophisticated secret agent brought together with the suave and sophisticated quintessentially British sports car. Throw in a mixture of improbable gadgetry and an arsenal of concealed weaponry and the result is a cinematic legend.

In 2012 the James Bond film franchise will have been motoring along for half a century. In that time 007 has appeared in a number of different makes of car, but it has been the Aston Martin that is most closely linked with the character to the extent that it is almost impossible to talk of one without mentioning the other. In no small part this was the result of some fortuitous timing. For Sean Connery's first on-screen appearance as Bond – *Dr No* released in 1962 – the story placed the action in Jamaica and the character in a standard Sunbeam Alpine convertible. In the second film, *From Russia with Love* (1963) he appeared with a Bentley Sports Tourer – a favourite of Bond's creator Ian Fleming. Elegant maybe, the Bentley was equipped with nothing more deadly than a telephone, and while this seemed like a very advanced piece of gadgetry at the time a mobile phone was hardly licensed

to thrill. The breakthrough moment came with *Goldfinger* which was released in 1964. The Bond films were already proving to be enormously popular and the film-makers took the opportunity to elevate the gadgetry to a central role within the plots.

In the *Goldfinger* novel, the seventh published although the third to be filmed, Fleming had given Bond an Aston Martin for the first time. Described in the book as a DB III, it was more likely a DB Mark III as the DB3 was intended specifically for racing. Fleming included all sorts of gadgets in the Bond novels, but this was the one and only time he fitted any to one of the cars. The special features included switches to alter the type and colour of the front and rear lights, in case Bond was being followed, reinforced steel bumpers to ram other vehicles, a tracking device and an assortment of concealed storage spaces including a compartment under

the driver's seat to hold a long-barrelled Colt 45.

When Ken Adam, production designer for the *Goldfinger* film, together with John Stears, the special effects supervisor, arrived at Aston Martin's works at Newport

◀ The most famous car in the world? Bond's DB5. (Ed Callow)

▼ Publicity photo of the definitive Bond with the definitive Bond car, the DB5 from *Goldfinger*.

Extending tyre slashers, of course. A control panel concealed under the armrest, naturally. And long before the world had heard of satnav, a screen for the Homer tracking device. (Ed Callow)

Worth its weight in gold, almost. The classic Corgi Toys James Bond DB5 diecast.

Pagnell in the autumn of 1963 they were captivated by the new Aston Martin DB5. Its curvaceous, yet muscular, styling represented the perfect vehicle for 007 and Stears set about loading the metallic silver DB5 with a very special bundle of optional

◀◀ Taking a Vantage, the 1985 V8 specifically, for *The Living Daylights*. Extending skis plus missiles behind the lights, the V8 Vantage also had laser beams, head-up display and a rocket booster. (JC)

◀ Pierce Brosnan's DB5 for *Goldeneye*, a softer shade of silver than Sean Connery's original. (JC)

extras. It was Q, played by actor Desmond Llewelyn, who introduced Bond to his new car with the legendary words, 'Now pay attention...' He then ran through the various modifications: 'Windscreen, bullet-proof, as are the side and rear windows. Revolving number plates, naturally, valid all countries...' The list continued with a transmitting device, called the Homer, together with a display screen concealed in the dashboard, a control panel hidden in the armrest with switches for the 'defence mechanisms' including smokescreen and oil slick, tyre slashers extending from the wheel hubs, a rear bullet-proof screen (surely superfluous as the windows were bullet-proof anyway) and front wing machine guns. Last, but by no means least, the top of the gear stick flipped open to reveal a red button to engage and fire the passenger ejector seat. Naturally each and every device just happened to be exactly the right one at a key moment in the story, and via Q's introductory spiel the film-makers raised the audience's anticipation throughout the film. The only disappointment with the DB5's performance in *Goldfinger* is that despite all the marvellous gadgetry Bond was tricked into crashing the car by a large mirror.

Ensuring true cult status, Corgi released an all-singing all-dancing die-cast model of the DB5. Finished in metallic gold, unlike the film version which was Silver Birch, it featured the retractable machine guns, telescopic over-riders, a rear bullet-proof shield and, best of all, the ejector seat with its tiny gun-toting villain figure who obligingly shot into the air and invariably disappeared without trace. Nevertheless, this toy car demonstrated the enormous value of film merchandising and launched a veritable industry in Bond car collectables.

The silvery DB5 appeared again in the next cinematic offering, *Thunderball*, which

was released in 1965. This time it featured only briefly as most of the action took place underwater. However, in the opening sequence Bond is seen escaping from a French château by jet-pack before fleeing in the Aston and releasing a torrent of water from concealed water cannon to foil his pursuers. (No explanation of what happened to the oil slick mechanism.)

Sean Connery's next Bond film, *You Only Live Twice*, was located in Japan and saw the Aston Martin usurped by the tiny Wallis autogyro, 'Little Nellie'. Connery then handed over to the once-only Bond actor George Lazenby for *On Her Majesty's Secret Service*. Lazenby's Bond drives a metallic-green Aston Martin DBS which appears in only four scenes including the shooting of his new bride, played by Diana Rigg. Obviously Q forgot the bullet-proof glass this time and the only gadget shown in the film is a gun compartment in the glove box. Following Lazenby's lacklustre performance, Sean Connery was persuaded to come back for a final time, officially at least, in *Diamonds Are Forever*. The DBS also returned but is glimpsed only fleetingly in Q's workshop where it is being fitted with rocket launchers and the car plays no part in the story.

Connery's departure marked a turning point in the Bond franchise. His replacement, Roger Moore, saw greater emphasis placed on the gags, and the long relationship with Aston Martins gave way to a dalliance with wedge-shaped Lotus Esprits. Moore played Bond for a record seven times, but by the time he retired from the role in 1985 the format was overdue for a make-over. Timothy Dalton was selected to play a more grounded Bond and to reinforce the image the Aston Martins were brought back. The 1987 film *The Living Daylights* actually featured two cars. The first was a V8 Vantage which was owned by Aston

Martin Lagonda chairman Victor Gauntlett; however, in later scenes this is 'winterised' by Q and morphs into a charcoal-grey V8 Volante. This vehicle sports some useful gadgetry including laser beams in the wheel hubs, retractable ski outriggers, bullet-proof windows, rocket launchers behind the front fog-lights and a jet engine for an extra power boost. Once again the controls were hidden in the armrest and, instead of a display screen, a heads-up system projected target information on to the windscreen. All good solid Bond fare. Late in the film Dalton activates the Volante's self-destruct mechanism, which partly explains why it doesn't appear in *Licence To Kill*, although this film also happens to be set in the USA.

Dalton's two appearances were followed by a six-year gap, caused by ongoing litigation, and by the time Bond returned to the screens in 1995's *Goldeneye* the role had been handed over to Pierce Brosnan.

The DB5 made a welcome return, albeit in a more muted silver grey, and is seen racing with a Ferrari in the opening sequence. The DB5 also makes a cameo appearances in *Tomorrow Never Dies* but the starring cars were the BMWs. In 2002 Ford, who owned Aston Martin at the time, signed a three-film deal with Eon who produce the Bond films. For *Die Another Day* Bond had a brand new Aston, and Q, now played by John Cleese, was on hand to explain: 'The ultimate in British engineering – Aston Martin call it the Vanquish, we call it the Vanish.' In what might have been a step too far for some purists, the Vanquish was equipped with adaptive camouflage which took images from tiny cameras to make it virtually invisible. But there were some old friends including an ejector seat, torpedoes, front-firing rockets and a pair of target-seeking guns that popped up from the bonnet grilles.

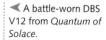

A battle-worn DBS V12 from *Quantum of Solace*.

Did you know?
Roger Moore was the only Bond never to drive an Aston Martin, but as Lord Brett Sinclair he drove a Bahama Yellow DBS, rebadged to look like the DBS V8, in the television series *The Persuader*.

Die Another Day was Brosnan's farewell performance as Bond and subsequently the character and timeline were reinvented for the Daniel Craig era. Fortunately Bond remains wedded to his Astons and the DB5 appears alongside the dark grey DBS in *Casino Royale* (2006), which returns in *Quantum of Solace* (2008).

The history of the individual cars used in making the Bond films is very convoluted as in many cases more than one car was used in any given film. For example, six DBS V12s were either damaged or written off in the making of the chase sequence in *Die Another Day* alone. Many of the surviving film cars are on public display at various museums, or appear in special exhibitions, while some are in the hands of lucky private collectors. In 2010 the DB5 driven by Sean Connery in both *Goldfinger* and *Thunderball*, which has been dubbed 'the most famous car in the world', sold at auction for £2.6 million.

SPORTS (DB1)

1950–1953	Aston Martin DB2
1953–1957	Aston Martin DB2/4
1957–1959	Aston Martin DB Mark III
1958–1963	Aston Martin DB4
1961–1963	Aston Martin DB4 GT Zagato
1963–1965	Aston Martin DB5
1965–1966	Aston Martin Short Chassis Volante
1965–1969	Aston Martin DB6
1967–1972	Aston Martin DBS
1969–1989	Aston Martin V8
1977–1989	Aston Martin V8 Vantage
1986–1990	Aston Martin V8 Zagato
1989–1996	Aston Martin Virage/Virage Volante
1989–2000	Aston Martin Virage
1993–2000	Aston Martin Vantage
1996–2000	Aston Martin V8 Coupé/V8 Volante

◄ David Brown Aston Martin plus the Aston Martin Owners' Club bonnet badge. (JC)

► Aston Martin threesome at the Haynes Motor Museum. (JC)

▲ Aston Martin DBS.
(Hatsukari715)

1993–2003	Aston Martin DB7/DB7 Vantage
2002–2003	Aston Martin DB7 Zagato
2002–2004	Aston Martin DB AR1
2001–2007	Aston Martin V12 Vanquish/Vanquish S
2004–	Aston Martin DB9
2005–	Aston Martin V8 and V12 Vantage

2007–	Aston Martin DBS V12
2009–	Aston Martin One-77
2010–	Aston Martin Rapide (four door)
2011–	Aston Martin Virage
2011	Cygnet, rebadged version of the Toyota iQ

OTHER NON-STANDARD MODELS

1944	Aston Martin Atom (concept)
1961–1964	Lagonda Rapide
1976–1989	Aston Martin Lagonda
1980	Aston Martin Bulldog
1993	Lagonda Vignale (concept)
2007	Aston Martin V12 Vantage RS (concept)
2007–2008	Aston Martin V8 Vantage N400
2008	Aston Martin Vanquish S
2009	Aston Martin Lagonda SUV (concept)
2010	Aston Martin V12 Vantage Carbon Black Edition
2010	Aston Martin DBS Carbon Black Edition

POST-WAR RACING CARS*

| 1950–1953 | Aston Martin DB3 |
| 1953–1956 | Aston Martin DB3S |

1956–1959	Aston Martin DBR1
1957–1958	Aston Martin DBR2
1958	Aston Martin DBR3
1959	Aston Martin DBR4
1960	Aston Martin DBR5
1962	Aston Martin DP212
1963	Aston Martin DP214
1963	Aston Martin DP215
1976–1979	Aston Martin RHAM/1
1989	Aston Martin AMR1
1989–1990	Aston Martin AMR2
2005–	Aston Martin DBR9
2005	Aston Martin DBRS9
2006	Aston Martin V8 Vantage N24
2006	Aston Martin V8 Vantage Rally GT
2008	Aston Martin V8 Vantage GT2
2008	Aston Martin V8 Vantage GT4
2009	Aston Martin DBR1-2
2011	Aston Martin AMR-One

*whole cars only

Aston Martin, by Schlegelmilch, Lehbank and von Osterroth, Ullman
 Publishing, 2010

Aston Martin – Power, Beauty and Soul, by David Dowsey, Images
 Publishing, 2010

Aston Martin – Ever the Thoroughbred, by Robert Edwards, 2009

The Ultimate History of Aston Martin, by Andrew Noakes, Marks &
 Spencer, 2003

Aston Martin – The Complete Story, by David Lillywhite, Dennis
 Publishing, 2009

Aston Martin – The Legend, by Michael Bowler, Paragon Plus, 1998

*The Most Famous Car in the World – Complete History of James Bond's
 Aston Martin DB5*, by Dave Worrall, Solo Publishing, 1993

WEBSITES

Aston Martin official website: www.astonmartin.com
Tim Cottingham's highly informative site: www.astonmartins.com
Aston Martin Owners Club: www.amoc.org
Aston Martin Heritage Trust: www.amht.org.uk

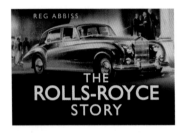

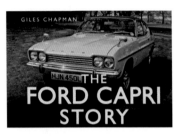

■ ISBN 978 07524 6614 9

■ ISBN 978 07524 8460 0

■ ISBN 978 07524 8461 7

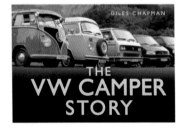

■ ISBN 978 07524 6281 3

■ ISBN 978 07524 5605 8

■ ISBN 978 07524 6404 6